THE
ULTIMATE
GUIDE TO
HOME
SECURITY

**How to
Select the Perfect
Door locks**

AKSHAT BANSAL

(ARCHITECTURAL HARDWARE EXPERT)

Worldwide Published by

Pendown Press

PENDOWN PRESS

An ISO 9001 & ISO 14001 Certified Co.,
Regd. Office: 2525/193, 1st Floor, Onkar Nagar-A,
Tri Nagar, Delhi-110035
Ph.: 09350849407, 09312235086
E-mail: info@pendownpress.com
Branch Office: 1A/2A, 20, Hari Sadan, Ansari Road,
Daryaganj, New Delhi-110002
Ph.: 011-45794768
Website: PendownPress.com

First Edition: 2021

ISBN: 978-93-91544-00-3

Layout and Cover Designed by Pendown Graphics Team
Printed and Bound in India by Thomson Press India Ltd.

"Good lock =
High Security =
Peace of Mind"

AKSHAT BANSAL
Architectural Hardware Expert

CONTENTS

SECTION 1

Chapter 1

Types of Locks   1

SECTION 2

Chapter 2

Types of Doors   15

FOREWORD

I first came across Akshat in the early 2000s as a young lad who had just joined his family hardware business. I met him at an exhibition, and I sought a door security solution for a very discerning client. During my first interaction, I discovered that many of the answers he provided were way beyond what anybody else in the market could even think of.

Akshat has encapsulated an entire experience of solutions related to door locks. He has created a 'must-have' manual for design professionals to enhance their knowledge and, as a result, offer great solutions to their clients. Readers will quickly become aware of all the possibilities regarding door lock choices and make informed decisions.

This no-nonsense, practical, and readily accessible book provides a perfect introduction for those wanting to learn more about selecting an ideal door lock and discovering the best solution for their home security. This book also provides an ideal stepping stone for finding more about door locks and offering the best technical solutions and recommendations.

–Daljit Singh

Creative Directive, Newage Concepts India (P) Ltd

FOREWORD

No matter how modern or aesthetically pleasing your project is, if it is not 100% secure for its users, then it's not a masterpiece yet.

In his latest book, Akshat Bansal (probably the Number 1. Expert in Architectural Hardware in India) has laid out practical strategies for adding solid security to your project and keeping users 100% safe.

A good read overall

–Akshar Yadav
(Creator Get Overbooked Framework)

INTRODUCTION

Hi, I am Akshat Bansal, an Architectural Hardware Expert with 18 years of experience.

My journey into this field of expertise began early on after receiving my Engineering Degree 18 years ago. I stepped into our family business in Chawri Bazar, in the heart of Old Delhi, Asia's largest Hardware market, with immense drive and bubbling enthusiasm to make a positive difference in people's lives.

Since then, I have been blessed with numerous opportunities to work with leading Architects and Interior Designers all over INDIA and provide them with the best hardware solutions.

My wife Minni often teases me that I eat, sleep and dream handles; I sleep handles to the power X, where obviously X=Infinity:). The situation is such that now even my daughter Pari jokes with me, saying, "Papa, can you just take a break and think of something else except handles and knobs":).

Handles have always been close to my heart; it's in my genes. Once you see the production, you can see a simple brass candle, getting the infusion of life by robotic machines and a handle is born. With state of the art Technological Advancements, it is truly inspirational to see Robots working and making door handles.

In my journey, I have helped many designers create magical interior spaces by selecting the world's best door handles and architectural hardware. It has been an incredible journey, and I have observed closely how attention to such small details can greatly impact the overall results.

Having worked with a lot of designers during my journey, I was able to see what a perfect door handle can do to interior spaces.

Also, I have realized that people are willing to spend on door handles as they are visible, but not on the locks, as they are hidden inside the door and are the least priority for most people. I don't mean that people want inferior locks, but they still don't want to invest in high-security locks.

This inspired me to share my knowledge so that designers and homemakers could use it effectively to make a perfect selection for a sound locking system for their doors, thereby adding high-Security to their homes and other buildings. This ultimately leads to peace of mind as you are assured of the safety of your loved ones and your valuable assets.

I am sure you are all eager to learn how to select the perfect door locks and get the high Security and Safety that you and your family deserve.

So without further ado, let's explore and dive in…

Your friend,

Architectural Hardware Expert.

– Akshat Bansal

To keep it simple, I have structured this book into 2 sections.

In Section 1, I will explain about the types of Locks so that you can understand what the most suitable lock options are.

In section 2, I will explain about the types of doors, and which types of locks are suitable for those based on the level of Security you require.

SECTION 1

Types of Locks:

1. **Multipoint Security Locks**

2. **Rim Locks or Night Latches**

3. **Mortise Lock and Cylinders**

4. **Sliding Door Locks**

5. **Digital Locks**

CHAPTER 1

TYPES OF LOCKS

1. Multipoint Security Locks

As the name suggests, a multipoint locking system locks at multiple points after the turn of a key, providing a high level of Security. Multipoint locking systems are commonly used on UPVC doors and are now becoming a standard for external timber doors.

The system will have a central deadbolt and 2-4 extra locking points to secure the door.

A key-operated multipoint lock system is fitted into the door's body and locks into the door frame.

When the lock is engaged, multiple bolts will engage into the door frame, usually with a minimum of 3 points and sometimes 4 or 5 points

The mechanism is usually operated with a euro cylinder lock to which the key inserts.

Advantages

The pros of having a multipoint lock as your door lock are:

- ✓ More locking points, so it's harder to force the door.
- ✓ Only one cylinder is required to lock the entire mechanism and can be keyed alike with other cylinder locks, so fewer keys are needed for one property
- ✓ Easy to change the cylinder or upgrade to a better standard cylinder.

Multipoint Locks only have One Lock Cylinder

You only have one lock cylinder; although this is convenient, it's fewer locks to defeat (a traditional wooden door may have 2 or more different locks on it).

These locks could be installed both with Lever handles and Pull handles.

These are the best locks for high levels of Security, not only for the main doors but also for back doors or terrace doors, that is to say, all the doors which open outside.

Please refer to the picture below for a 3 point lock:

2. Rim Locks or Night Latches

A Night Latch is a lock commonly found on the front doors of homes; they are mounted to the inner surfaces of doors that open inwards. When the door is closed, the night latch automatically latches the door shut.

The door can be kept from latching closed by keeping the door 'on the latch', a phrase you may have heard of.

Night Latches are very simple Security devices; they are easy to use. Open the door with a key and shut the door behind you.

Please find below some pictures of Common Night latches available in the market:

3. Mortise Locks and Cylinders

A mortise lock is a very strong, unique locking system fitted to the inside of a door. To use a mortise lock, your door must be thick enough to accommodate it. The minimum door width is 45mm or 1.75 inches. If you want to improve your door security, just know that this type of lock offers far better protection against intruders than the standard cylinder locks.[1]

Reasons to use a Mortise Lock?

Here are four primary reasons why you would want to use a mortise lock over other lock types:

✓ Burglars prefer to break in through doors, so improved door security is paramount

✓ Mortise locks are reliable and robust, thus offering good door security

✓ The classical appearance makes them more attractive than cylinder locks

✓ They're versatile so that you can use them with all kinds of door furniture and cylinders

How Do Mortise Locks Work?

The mortise lock has to fit neatly into the mortise cut-out, or pocket, made in the door. There are four essential parts to the lock:

- The mortise lock (latent once installed)

- The lock trim (door lever, doorknob or door handle)

- The strike plate (metal lining for the hole within the door frame)

- The keyed cylinder (it's where the lock and unlock function occurs)

The housing for the bolt is the 'lock body'. This is where the mechanical components are situated that engage and disengage the actual lock. These components include:

- A Mortise cylinder

- A Deadbolt (bolt only), or

- Sashlocks (a door catch plus a locking bolt)

- A Dead latch

- A Latch bolt

The door handles or door knobs turn to withdraw the latch once the door's unlocked. There's also the 'through-spindle'. This is simply the long rod that links the door handle or knob to the mortise lock body. A threaded 'lock cylinder' lets you unlock the door once you insert the key. The 'cam' component is a rectangular piece of metal that rotates to retract the door latch. The size and weight of a mortise lock mean they can withstand considerable usage. Please note that because there's quite a bit going on inside a mortise lock, they need simple servicing periodically.

Doors Best Suited to Mortise Locks

Almost all burglars and intruders will try to enter a residence from the front door of a property. Needless to say, this is your priority door when it comes to home security. All the same, if you have other entrance doors, you might want to consider using the locks on those too. Not all burglars 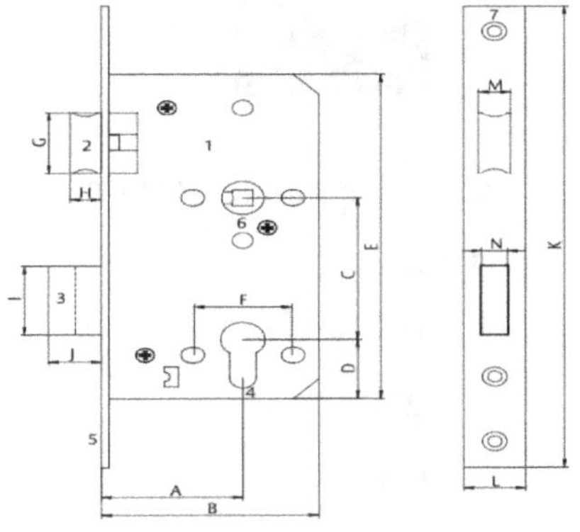 give up if they can't break in via the front door, which is why it is essential to keep all entrance doors secured.

If you want to replace your existing handle set, you need to take careful measurements as not all mortise boxes have the same dimensions. If you currently have cylinder type hardware on your door, it is possible to replace it with mortise hardware, but not all mortise boxes will cover the tubular holes already drilled in your door. Our hardware expert will be happy to talk with you and assist you in finding something that will fit your needs.

Please find the pictures of essential Mortise locks and cylinders below:

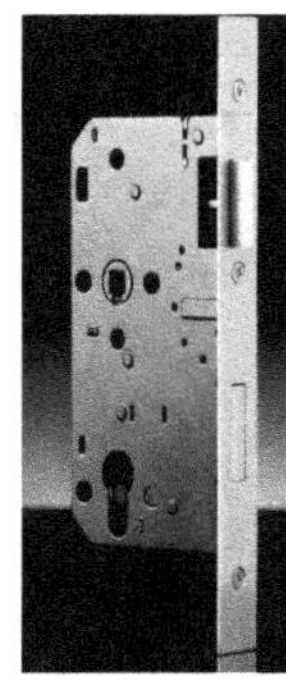 

Parts of a Lock explained:

Parts:

- Lock case
- Latch bolt
- Deadbolt
- Euro cylinder hole
- Face plate
- Lever follower
- Counter sunk holes

Types of Cylinders

Euro cylinder locks explained: Euro Cylinder Locks come in three options, keyed on both sides, half euro keyed only on one side and thumb turn. These options give you various degrees of Security and convenience – choose whichever suits you and your needs. For instance, if you like the idea of just having to lock your door from one side, then the half euro cylinder is best for you.

- Keyed Both Sides
- Thumbturn Cylinder
- Half Euro Cylinder

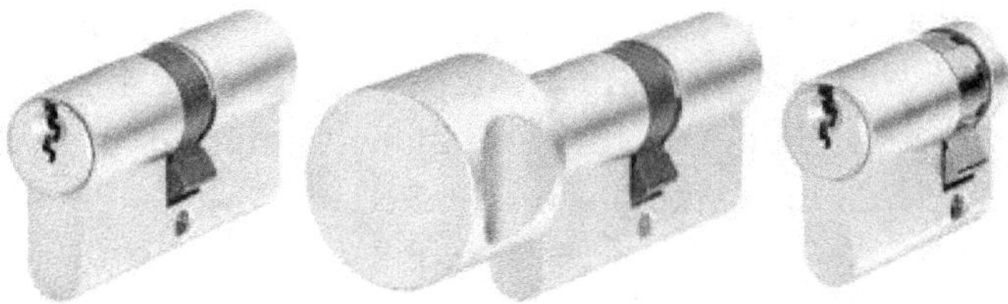

What Size Cylinder?

With the help of the diagram below, I have explained how to measure the size of the cylinder you need.

Euro Cylinder Diagram

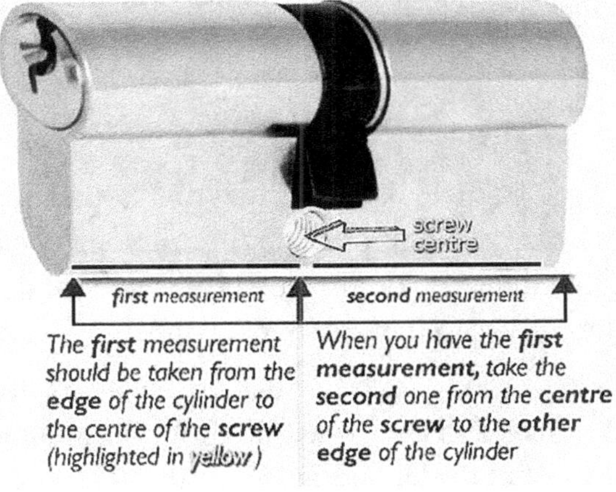

The **first measurement** should be taken from the edge of the cylinder to the centre of the **screw** (highlighted in yellow)

When you have the **first measurement**, take the **second** one from the **centre** of the **screw** to the **other edge** of the cylinder

Please refer to this 'How To Measure Your Euro Cylinder Lock' diagram.

The first measurement should be taken from the edge of the cylinder to the centre of the screw.

The second measurement should be taken from the centre of the screw to the other edge of the cylinder.

4. Sliding Door Lock

Cylindrical sliding locks are used for locking the sliding doors. The cylindrical sliding door lock can be installed in heavy doors and doors with more than 40mm thickness where star key deadlocks cannot be installed.

5. Digital Locks

If you've ever been locked out of your home because you forgot your keys, you'll appreciate the convenience of keyless locks. Digital door locks are powered by batteries and are popular alternatives to the standard key and lock combination.

They are one of the best security systems for modern homes and offices and can be acquired for all budgets ranging from 8000 to 60000, depending upon the features.

Types of Digital Door Locks

When choosing a digital lock for your home, consider the application method that best suits your family.

There are a few main types of digital locks, with some offering a combination of ways you can unlock them.

Password Digital Door Locks

Password digital locks are one of the most common types due to their simplicity and affordability. Simply set a password to be used to enter your home or office.

A keypad/combination lock model requires a PIN to unlock the door. They are very easy to install and maintain, and you can assign different codes to different users. You can change the PIN at any time, allowing you to manage access to your building easily.

Some models have protective mechanisms such as keypads that shut down after an incorrect code has been entered three times. Most newer models have a touch screen, but some have physical buttons. There are also combination keypad locks, which use a PIN in conjunction with another type of lock, such as deadbolts or handles.

PROS

✓ You don't need to carry a key/card

CONS

✗ You need to remember the password

Biometric Digital Door Locks

Because of the added Security they offer, biometric digital door locks are quickly gaining popularity. To set it up, you'll need to register your fingerprint so that it can recognize you.

Biometric locks are a popular, up-and-coming electronic door lock option. You can unlock a door by having your fingerprint or (less commonly) your eye scanned. This is a very secure option since fingerprints are all unique and are very difficult to forge. It's also a convenient option for individuals who don't have to carry a key fob with them, which means they always have access.

Biometric door locks work by scanning a fingerprint and converting it into a numerical template, telling the system to unlock the door. Because this system is so dependent on connectivity, look for a model with a backup option like a keypad or mechanical lock so you can still gain entry if your fingerprint cannot be scanned.

Many models have a limit of 100 fingerprints that can be stored, so if your company is larger, a biometric lock may not be the best option for you.

This is more secure than a password as it can't be copied or shared.

PROS

✓ You don't need to carry a key/card

✓ Passwords can't be shared

CONS

✗ Fingerprints need to be registered beforehand

Bluetooth Digital Door Locks

Bluetooth locks require your mobile phone to be within range to be connected. The lock grants you access when it's synced with your device.

One disadvantage is the inability to access the lock when your phone is out of battery.

Keyless and wireless smart locks are some of the most popular options. They allow you to connect to your locks over a Wi-Fi connection so that you can control your locks from anywhere in the world via a mobile app or remote. However, unless you purchase your locks as part of a smart home package, they may not come with a dedicated mobile app.

Many smart locks offer Bluetooth capability, which can automatically unlock your doors once you get within a certain distance. You may also be able to use your phone or a key fob and tap the sensor to unlock the door.

PROS

✓ Able to access and customize all functionalities of the lock through the mobile app.

CONS

✗ Unable to unlock the door without your phone, or if the phone runs out of battery.

CARD/RFID Digital Door Locks

A card is placed at the reader for verification before access is granted. Cards and RFID locks are commonly used in offices and commercial buildings because different access levels can be granted to each group of users.

Key fobs or key cards are a way to unlock your Bluetooth or radio frequency identification (RFID)-enabled smart lock. You simply tap the fob or card against the lock sensor to disarm it. Key fobs and cards can be programmed to unlock multiple locks, so, for example, your one key fob can let you into the front, side and office doors in your building.

PROS

✓ Ability to activate and deactivate any number of cards

CONS

✗ Will be locked out if cards are misplaced or forgotten

How to choose an electronic keyless door lock

When choosing a keyless lock, the first thing to determine is which type of lock suits your business best. A keypad lock often works well if you don't want to give people physical keys, fobs or access cards.

You must consider how many codes you will need; many models are limited by the number of codes they can support. You also need to decide if you need a dedicated mobile app that allows you to lock or unlock your doors, receive mobile alerts, or control your locks remotely.

The next step is to determine which features are must-haves and which features you can do without. Last, what type of credentials do you want – key fobs, a smartphone app, key cards, or something else?

Low-battery indicator

No matter which type of keyless door lock you choose, look for one that has a low-battery indicator that alerts you when the battery needs to be replaced. Some models have an indicator light that appears, whereas, with other locks, it might have a slower response time or require multiple attempts to open the door. This is an important feature because it will help you avoid being locked out due to a dead battery.

Integrations

Consider which integrations you'll need. Many people like to integrate their door locks with Alexa, Google Home, IFTTT, Wink or Smart Things, but not all locks can do that. Also, consider whether you need the lock to be integrated with a security system and/or connected to video surveillance systems, cameras, alarms and more.

SECTION 2

Types of Doors:

1. **Main Doors**
2. **Bedroom/Living Room Doors**
3. **Bathroom Doors**
4. **Balcony Doors**
5. **Sliding Doors**

CHAPTER 2

TYPES OF DOORS

1. Main Doors

The main doors of a house are the most important when we talk about the home's Security, as that's the first thing that needs to be the most secure.

Also, the type of locks you should use will depend on what type of Handles you are using for the Doors.

As we are talking about Security, I will be explaining the main door locks options sorted from Highest security to lower ones.

So here are the types of locks you should consider for Main Doors:

1. Multipoint Security Locks
2. Night Latches
3. Mortise Locks with Cylinders
4. Digital Locks

Primarily these are the 4 types of locks that should be used for the main doors; I have ranked them as per the level of Security, so Ideally, Multipoint locks provide the highest Security, second comes the night latches, third the mortise locks and cylinders and fourth are the digital locks.

2. Bedroom/Living Room Doors

Bedroom/Living Room doors are the second most important doors when it comes to Security in the house.

So here are the types of locks you should consider for Bedroom/Living Room Doors:

1. Mortise Locks with Cylinders
2. Digital Locks

Mortise locks and cylinders are the most used for internal doors, and for these doors, the ideal cylinder would be with one side key and one side knob as it's easy to open and lock the doors from inside with the help of the knob inside. This also eliminates the need for a Tower Bolt.

Digital locks are only suggested if there is a high need for Security for the bedroom door, if you have valuables in your bedroom, else it is not required. It gives an added advantage of keyless entry as usually people forget to keep the keys of bedroom doors handy.

3. Bathroom Doors

Bathroom doors are similar to bedroom doors, so the same mortise lock and cylinders are advised. This also helps keep the look, feel and aesthetics the same for the internal doors and gels well with the interiors giving your space a cohesive and finished feel.

4. Balcony Doors

Balcony Doors are ideally as critical as the house's main doors from the security point of view.

So ideally extra care should be taken for a good amount of Security for these doors.

Usually, mortise lock bodies and cylinders are suitable for these doors. Still, a special cylinder called the half-cylinder is the best for such doors, as then there are no keyholes on the outside, which mean higher Security as a thief won't have access to the cylinder to break in.

Also, depending on the situation, if there are some back entry doors, balcony doors, or terrace doors that need extra Security, multipoint locks could be an option to consider. Of course, it all depends on the situation.

5. Sliding Doors

Sliding Door locks are the best for Sliding doors as all the sliding locks have a hook type bolt which is apt for locking the sliding doors.

While sharing my expertise on locks and Security in this book, I have tried my best to keep it simple so that everyone can understand and use this knowledge for enhancing Security and selecting the best locks for their homes.

Though there are many more specialized types of locks that you may find for special applications, they are not relevant to a majority of the people, so I have not discussed them in this book.

It is my sincere intention and belief that this book will help you select a good lock, thereby adding the much-needed Security to your space and giving you peace of mind.

So here is a quick recap of what I have shared in this book.

CALL TO ACTION

Now you have 2 choices: go in the market and select the best locks for your doors armed with the knowledge I have shared, and I am sure now you will be able to choose the perfect door locks for your doors and make your homes more secure.

But if you feel you will not be able to get the best choices in the market, I am always there to help you; you can visit my online store Benzoville Hardware **www.benzoville.com** or visit my showroom in Delhi or Gurgaon.

Benzoville is a Delhi based importer of Premium quality Designer Door Hardware and Fittings. The company's customers range from interior designers & architects to homeowners as well. If you are looking for a wide variety of collections of door handles to choose from, please visit our website **www.benzoville.com.**

If you want suggestions or help in selecting the best door locks for your home or office, please share your Door Images on Whatsapp: **Akshat Bansal– 9810406140,** and I will surely get back to you with a perfect solution.

www.ingramcontent.com/pod-product-compliance
Lightning Source LLC
Chambersburg PA
CBHW070328160726
47999CB00003B/1204